W9-BYL-488

MONSTERS

THE LOCH NESS MONSTER

MONSTERS

THE LOCH NESS MONSTER

BY PEGGY J. PARKS

KIDHAVEN PRESS
An imprint of Thomson Gale, a part of The Thomson Corporation

THOMSON
✳
GALE™

Detroit • New York • San Francisco • San Diego • New Haven, Conn.
Waterville, Maine • London • Munich

Picture Credits

Cover: © Victor Habbick Visions/Photo
  Researchers, Inc.
Courtesy of Kirk Bauer, 35
© Chris Butler/Photo Researchers, Inc., 30
  (above)
© MC Pherson Colin/CORBIS SYGMA, 37
© Vo Trung Dung/CORBIS SYGMA, 27
© Fortean Picture Library, 9 (above), 17
  (below)
© Getty Images, 38
© Victor Habbick Visions, 7, 10-11, 16
© Austin Hepburn/Fortean Picture Library, 20

© Keystone/Stringer/Getty Images, 19
© Rafael Macia/Photo Researchers, Inc.,
  33
Mary Evans Picture Library, 24 (above),
  34
© Ivor Newby/Fortean Picture Library, 17
  (above)
Brandy Noon, 28
© Reuters/CORBIS, 30 (below)
© Anthony Shiels/Fortean Picture Library, 24
  (below)
Topham/The Image Works, 13
© Andreas Trottmann/Fortean Picture
  Library, 9 (below)

For more information, contact
KidHaven Press
27500 Drake Rd.
Farmington Hills, MI 48331-3535
Or you can visit our Internet site at http://www.gale.com

LIBRARY OF CONGRESS CATALOGING-IN-PUBLICATION DATA

Parks, Peggy J., 1951-
  The Loch Ness monster / by Peggy J. Parks.
    p. cm. — (Monsters)
  Includes bibliographical references and index.
  ISBN 0-7377-3166-4 (hard cover : alk. paper)
  1. Loch Ness monster—Juvenile literature. I. Title. II. Monsters series
(KidHaven Press)
  QL89.2L6P37 2005
  001.944–dc22

2004023594

CONTENTS

CHAPTER 1

THE LEGEND OF NESSIE

In an area of Scotland known as the Scottish Highlands, there is a lake called Loch Ness. It is a massive body of water: 24 miles (39km) long and more than a mile (1.6km) wide. The **loch** (the Scottish word for "lake") is surrounded by tree-covered mountains and steep banks. It is also ancient. It was carved out of the Earth by glaciers thousands of years ago. The water in the loch is pitch black. In fact, it is impossible to see more than a foot or two below the surface. The water is very cold, and in some places it is up to 800 feet

Opposite: This computer-generated illustration shows Nessie, the mysterious beast that is said to live in Scotland's Loch Ness.

(244m) deep. Shrouded in morning mist, the loch has a mysterious aura about it. The real mystery is not its enormous size, its black water, or its mist, however. It is the beast that is said to live there: Nessie, the Loch Ness Monster.

Saint Columba's Story

The earliest known encounter with the beast of Loch Ness is described in the biography of an Irish monk named Saint Columba. In A.D. 565, as he stood on the shores of the loch, he saw a man swimming. He then noticed a large creature emerging from the water. It was speeding toward the man with its mouth open. Columba heard the beast roar, and he knew the man was about to be attacked. He raised his hand and made the sign of the cross in the air. In a loud, commanding voice he ordered the beast, in the name of God, not to touch the man. He then told it to retreat back into the water. The beast obeyed him. It disappeared into the depths of the loch, and the swimmer's life was spared.

Several astonished people witnessed this event and told others about it. One hundred years after Columba's death, Saint Adamnan wrote his biography. It included an account of the monk's triumph over the fearsome loch creature. Because Columba had been a revered religious man, his word was not questioned.

Over the following centuries, other people told of encounters with the beast of Loch Ness. It was

 The Loch Ness Monster

The biography of Saint Columba (left) tells the story of the saint's encounter with the creature in the year 565.

described by some as a sea serpent, and by others as a monstrous fish or water horse. Eventually, the creature became known as Nessie.

A HUGE CREATURE WITH HUMPS

Most stories about the beast were considered Scottish folklore rather than fact. Scientists scoffed at the idea that such a creature could exist. Then in 1933, a new road was built along the Loch Ness shoreline. It provided a much clearer view of the water. Suddenly, reports of Nessie sightings began to soar.

Everyone who told of the beast had a slightly different story. There were many similarities, though.

NESSIE CHARACTERISTICS

Over the years people have described the Loch Ness Monster in many different ways. Below are examples of how Nessie might look.

Long, thin neck and horselike head; shy temperament

Gray or black in color

Powerful whalelike flippers

Long, lizardlike tail

Green brown color

11

For instance, it was almost always described as either large or enormous. Some people estimated the creature's size to be about 20 feet (6.1m) long. Others thought it was much larger, perhaps as much as 50 feet (15m) long. It was said to resemble a dinosaur, with a long neck and a small, horselike head. A few observers reported seeing a long tail, as one person noted: "I saw the tail distinctly causing a great commotion, thrashing the water with much force."[1] Many people saw humps on the creature's back. Some described the humps as round, while others insisted they were triangular. Aside from Columba's encounter, no one described the beast as fierce or dangerous. It just kept to itself and did not bother anyone. Almost everyone said it was in the water, and some reported seeing flippers.

In May 1933, an account by Mr. and Mrs. John McKay was published in a newspaper called the *Inverness Courier.* In the article, the writer referred to a "monster" in the loch. He wrote that the couple had observed it "rolling and plunging for fully a minute, its body resembling that of a whale, and the water cascading and churning like a simmering cauldron. Soon, however, it disappeared in a boiling mass of foam."[2]

A few months later, there was a different sort of report. The beast had been spotted on land. The couple who saw it were Mr. and Mrs. Spicer. In a letter to the newspaper, Mr. Spicer said they had seen an "extraordinary form of an animal crossing the road. . . . It did not move in the usual reptilian fashion but . . . it shot across the road until a ponderous body about four feet high came into view."[3] He described the beast as dark gray in color, with a long neck a little thicker than an elephant's trunk. The Spicers both thought the creature resembled an enormous snail.

World-Famous Photograph

Although many people reported seeing Nessie, no one had any real proof that the monster existed. They had only their own personal stories to tell. Some produced photos that they claimed showed the monster. None were good enough to convince nonbelievers that there really was a monster. The photos were either too fuzzy or were obvious fakes.

In 1934, a physician named R. Kenneth Wilson produced a photograph of what he said was the Loch Ness Monster. According to Wilson, he was driving along the shore when he heard a great commotion in the water. Upon hearing the noise, he turned and saw an enormous beast emerge from the loch. He grabbed his camera and captured it on film. The photo

This 1934 photo convinced many people that Nessie is real. The photo was later proved to be a fake.

appeared in the *London Daily Mail* newspaper on April 21, 1934. It clearly showed a large dinosaurlike creature with a long neck and small head. Wilson's name, and his photograph, became famous.

Few people doubted that the photograph was real. Even some who had been skeptical about the Loch Ness Monster began to wonder if they had been mistaken. The man who had taken the photo was a well-respected surgeon from London. There was no reason to believe he would make up the story, or create a fake photograph. Why would a reputable man do such a thing?

Sixty years after the photo was published, that question was answered. A man named Alastair Boyd did some detective work. He and another scientist discovered that Wilson had been part of an elaborate hoax. The "beast" shown swimming in Loch Ness was not a real beast at all. It was a toy submarine with a molded monsterlike neck and head attached to the top. What the photo actually showed was the toy floating in the loch. Newspapers all over the world quickly exposed it as a fake.

Boyd's findings did not make him a popular person. Many Scottish people were angry with him. Some claimed he had made the story up. They said he, not Wilson, was responsible for the *real* hoax. They even began calling him "the Nessie killer." After nurturing the Loch Ness mystery for nearly fifteen hundred years, people deeply resented the man who tried to destroy it.

The Loch Ness Monster

Chapter 2

"Heavens Above! I've Actually Seen It!"

Boyd did not appreciate being called "the Nessie killer." He was especially disturbed because he believed in the monster. In 1979, he was on the shores of Loch Ness when he spotted what he described as an unknown animal in the water. The part of the body he could see looked to be about 20 feet (6m) long. Then he saw the "large, powerful creature turn around, just under the surface, and then a large, dark hump came heaving out of the water, rolling forward . . . like a whale;

This computer-generated image shows Nessie's long neck as the monster breaks the surface of the water.

it was there for several seconds."[4] Boyd said it was the most amazing thing he had ever seen. He added: "If I could afford to spend the rest of my life looking for another glimpse of it, I would."[5]

NESSIE IN THE MOVIES

Nearly twenty years before Boyd's sighting of the creature, another scientist had captured it on film. His name was Tim Dinsdale. He had read a book called *More than a Legend* by a Scottish doctor named Constance Whyte. The book contained numerous eyewitness reports, as well as sketches of the beast. After reading it, Dinsdale became fascinated with the Loch Ness Monster. In April 1960 he traveled to the

The Loch Ness Monster

Scottish Highlands. He planned to spend a week there to try to get a glimpse of the beast.

Toward the end of his visit, Dinsdale got his wish. He was standing on a hilltop overlooking the loch. The light of day had begun to fade, but he kept his movie camera focused on the water below. Suddenly he saw what he described as "a violent disturbance— a churning ring of rough water, [centering] about what appeared to be two long black shadows, or shapes, rising and falling in the water!"[6] He caught the action on camera and was convinced it was the swimming monster. Two days later he saw the beast again. This time his encounter was much more exciting. Watching through binoculars, he observed that the creature was enormous.

Scientist Tim Dinsdale claimed to have filmed Nessie swimming in the loch in 1960.

It had a huge hump on its back and was reddish brown in color. He dropped the binoculars, grabbed his movie camera, and began filming the beast as it swam. He later wrote: "I watched successive rhythmic bursts of foam break the surface—*paddle strokes:* with such a regular beat I instinctively began to count—one, two, three, four—pure white blobs of froth contrasting starkly against the black water."[7]

Dinsdale provided his film to the Joint Air Reconnaissance Intelligence Center of the British Armed Forces. Some experts at the center specialized in examining photography. They confirmed that the film was genuine and that there was definitely something "animate" in the water. It was their opinion that the object (or creature) was no less than 6 feet wide, 5 feet high, and 16 feet long (1.8m wide, 1.5m high, and 4.9m long).

"A WONDERFUL CREATURE"

Dinsdale's monster movie was shown on British television. Before long, people all over the world became interested in the beast of Loch Ness. One woman who had seen the film on television wrote to Dinsdale. Her name was Marjory Moir, and she lived in Inverness, near the loch. She told of something she had experienced nearly twenty-five years before. She and some family members were driving along the shore when they saw a "wonderful creature." It was about 30 feet (9m) long, with a long, slender neck and three humps on its back.

She explained how they had watched in amazement: "The creature was quite stationary, and often dipped its head into the water, either feeding or amusing itself . . . then suddenly it swung round away from the shore, and shot across the loch at a terrific speed, putting up a wash exactly similar to that I saw in your film."[8] Along with her letter, Moir enclosed a sketch she had drawn. She wrote that the beast was obviously very powerful and graceful, and that it was thrilling to see it. She also made it clear that many other people had seen the creature too.

Throughout the 1960s, more sightings were reported–forty in 1963 alone. Two years later, a retired police detective named Ian Cameron reportedly

In 1969 a member of a research team searches for signs of Nessie.

Opposite: This sequence of photos shows an unidentified creature swimming in the loch in 1996.

encountered the beast. On a summer day he was fishing in Loch Ness when he noticed something break the surface of the water. He continued to watch the spot and observed a large, black object that looked like a whale. Cameron later said that if he had not seen it himself, he would not have believed it: "In no way am I even attempting to convert anybody to the religion of the object of Loch Ness. I mean, they can believe it, but it doesn't upset me if they don't believe it. . . . But I saw it, and nothing can take that away."[9] His friend saw the beast at the same time, as did a group of people watching from the opposite shore.

"IT MUST HAVE BEEN THE MONSTER"

Another man who often fished in the loch was Ronald Mackintosh. He has a vivid memory of his encounter with the Loch Ness Monster. It happened when he was fourteen. He recalls driving with his brother and mother toward Inverness. Suddenly he looked toward the water and shouted to his mother to stop the car. In the center of the loch, they could see a massive creature. He said it was a grayish brown color, and he described its actions: "Now, I always try to relate it to the size of a bus, a big bus. It flipped over, just flipped right over like that, crashed down. You could see it. . . .

That's what I actually saw with my own eyes and my late mother saw and my late brother saw. . . . It was an object, it was huge. What was it? It must have been the monster."[10]

"Oh, There's Nessie"

In recent years, people have continued to report seeing the Loch Ness Monster. Val Moffatt, who lives on the shores of the loch, recalls seeing the beast in 1990. She glanced at the water and saw what looked like an upside-down boat, as she explains: "About 30 feet in length, and nearly 10 feet in height from the water to the top of the back. . . . It was a mixture of browns, greens, sludgy sort of colors. . . . Well, I thought to myself, 'Oh, there's Nessie. 'Bout time I saw it. . . .' And then something in the back of my head sort of said, 'That's . . . got to be *the* Loch Ness Monster . . . and you're looking at the darn thing.'"[11]

Gary Campbell is an Inverness resident who tells of his own experience. In March 1996 he was sitting beside the loch doing paperwork. Out of the corner of his eye, he noticed something come up out of the water. When he looked toward the object, he could see that it was a black hump. It went below the surface of the water, came back up, and then went back down. He knew it was not any sort of fish or seal. Rather, it was a creature like nothing he had ever seen before. He remembers thinking: "I've seen it! Good grief, after all these years being here. . . . Heavens above! I've actually seen it!"[12]

The Loch Ness Monster

CHAPTER 3

REALITY OR MYTH?

ameron, Campbell, Moffatt, and many others are convinced that the Loch Ness Monster exists. They believe in the creature because they say they have seen it with their own eyes. They are certainly not alone. Over the years there have been hundreds, or even thousands, of sightings. Could all these people be mistaken? Yes, say the skeptics, there is no such beast living in the loch. Their theory is that humans often see whatever they want to see.

NESSIE? OR A BOAT?

One of the biggest sources of controversy has been Tim Dinsdale's movie. Although he died in 1987, people who knew him say he was a man who truly

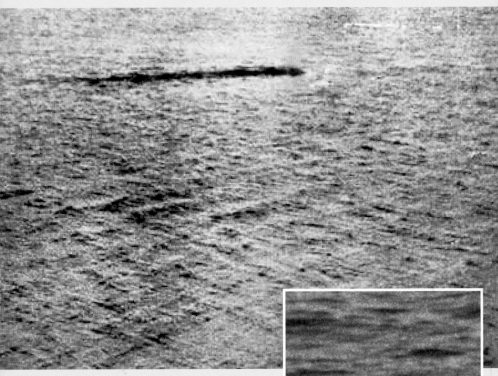

Even dramatic photos like these fail to convince skeptics that a monster lives in Loch Ness.

believed in the Loch Ness Monster. He devoted more than twenty years of his life to hunting for it. Yet some of those who have studied the film believe Dinsdale made a mistake. They say that the object in his movie was a boat. After enlarging frames of the movie, they noticed a small white blob on the back of the moving object. They believe it was a man driving the boat.

Scientist and university professor Henry Bauer disagrees. He, too, has studied the film, and he insists the object is a creature. A hump can be seen going under the water, but the **wake** continues behind it. He believes that means something huge was moving below the surface. Bauer explains the significance of this: "In the last portion, the wake moves right to left and one can see no solid object above the water, but there are periodic splashes at the side, like oar strokes. These are probably signs of limbs moving. What else could they be? What else could have produced this wake and earlier hump? Only some large animal, it seems to me."[13]

Theories Galore

Many of those who do not believe in the Loch Ness Monster acknowledge that people have seen something. They just do not believe it was a monster. Jonathan Downes, for instance, has theories about the beast. Downes is a **cryptozoologist**. He studies creatures that may exist but that are not accepted by formal science. Downes's theory is that Nessie actually may be a giant eel. He says sometimes eels stay in bodies of freshwater, instead of swimming into the open sea. As a result, they keep eating and growing until they become huge. He explains: "As long as something doesn't get them first, there's no real size limit—a few years ago an 18-foot long eel was found in a ship canal. . . . If you ask me, Nessie is a bloody great 30-foot-long eel."[14] Others have suggested that the beast is a type of primitive fish known as a Baltic sturgeon, or perhaps an oversize river otter. Other possible explanations of what the beast could be include tree trunks, shadows, and huge masses of vegetation.

Some scientists say there is no creature, but **natural phenomena** caused it to look like there was. For instance, Luigi Piccardi, a geologist from Florence, Italy, says **seismic** energy, or shock waves within the Earth, could cause such a vision. Even seismic activity far away from a body of water can create enormous waves. In 1755, a major earthquake in Portugal resulted in an enormous sloshing wave, called a **seiche**, on Loch Ness. Piccardi notes that many eyewitnesses have reported great commotions on the loch. He believes seismic activity could fool them into thinking the commotions were caused by a water beast. Geologists who share Piccardi's viewpoint say the "monster sightings" were probably nothing more than nature playing tricks on people's eyes.

INVESTIGATIVE WORK

The doubters have some very convincing arguments about why Nessie cannot possibly exist. Over the years, however, many people have worked hard to prove them wrong. Various groups have been created to find the mysterious creature. The first formal group was the Loch Ness Phenomena Investigation Bureau, formed in 1962. The Bureau, as it was

134

WILLIAMSON

Fig 4. Seal making successive jumps, as seen by fisherman Mr G

. 5. A Common Seal jumping in sea near Orkney Islands. Photograph by Paul
hompson.

le – noticed the seal. Common Seals spend
urface, and make dives of 3–8 minute
onclusion: in Loch Ness it is
less you spend many
athed in and o
fall of

This photo shows how a seal swimming in Loch Ness might easily be mistaken for Nessie.

Reality or Myth?

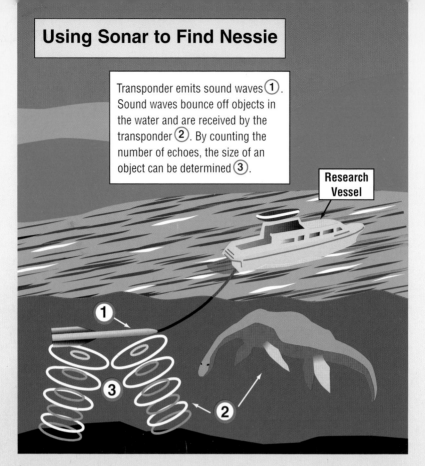

Using Sonar to Find Nessie

Transponder emits sound waves (1). Sound waves bounce off objects in the water and are received by the transponder (2). By counting the number of echoes, the size of an object can be determined (3).

Research Vessel

known, had one mission: to seek evidence that would prove the monster was real.

Bureau members set up camp on the Loch Ness shoreline. They lived in trailers and took turns watching the water through binoculars. They kept watch from dawn to dusk, waiting and hoping. Often they used searchlights to illuminate the water after dark. They had still cameras and movie cameras ready, just in case. If anyone saw a disturbance of any kind, he or she was prepared to capture it on film. The group worked on the project for ten years, but never accomplished anything considered significant.

The Loch Ness Monster

In 1972, the Bureau partnered with a scientific group from Boston. They planned several expeditions led by Robert Rines. Their boats had underwater cameras that could take pictures every forty-five seconds. The boats also had **sonar** equipment, which would scour the loch with sound waves. If the waves encountered any large objects, echoes would bounce back to the sonar sending device, called a **transponder**. The size of the object could then be determined by counting the number of echoes.

Over the next three years, the group made some unusual discoveries. During one expedition, the sonar recorded something that was very large and moving. At the same time, cameras photographed flipperlike objects that were from 6 to 8 feet (2 to 3m) long. Close-up photos taken on another expedition showed what looked like the head and body of a large creature. In both cases, scientists examined the photos and sonar readings. They confirmed that there could be some sort of large, unknown aquatic beast in the loch. Nonbelievers, however, scoffed at the reports. They continued to insist that there was no proof of a monster.

THE FINAL WORD?

There were a few scientists who had theories about the images. They said the creature could possibly be an ancient aquatic reptile known as a **plesiosaur**. The scientists knew it was highly unlikely

Gerald McSorley (right) discovered fossilized vertebrae from a plesiosaur (above) near the loch in 2003.

that this was the case. Plesiosaurs lived in warm tropical seas, and the water in the loch was icy cold. Besides, the animals had been extinct for millions of years. Still, the scientists wondered if one ple-

The Loch Ness Monster

siosaur had somehow managed to survive. If so, perhaps it had taken up residence in Loch Ness.

In July 2003, it looked as though the theory might be true. A Scottish man named Gerald McSorley found a large fossil in the loch that belonged to an ancient plesiosaur. He later said, "I have always believed in the Loch Ness monster, but this proves it for me. The resemblance between this and the sightings which have been made are so similar."[15] McSorley's discovery turned out to be a hoax. The fossil was indeed that of a plesiosaur. However, scientists who examined it could tell it had been taken from somewhere else, probably from an area close to the ocean. It had likely been left in Loch Ness for some unsuspecting person to find.

The same month the fossil was found, the British Broadcasting Corporation (BBC) launched an aggressive expedition. Boats equipped with hundreds of sonar beams scoured Loch Ness. The researchers on the mission were not among the skeptics. They believed there was a creature in the loch, and they hoped to find it. Their search found no trace of a beast, however. Even if the Loch Ness Monster existed in the past, the BBC team was convinced it was now gone.

CHAPTER 4

NESSIE'S LEGACY

Whether people believe in the Loch Ness Monster or not, the creature is famous. The words *Loch Ness* can hardly be spoken without someone thinking about the monster. Scottish schoolchildren sing a song called "I Saw the Loch Ness Monster." Hotels and visitor centers on the loch greet people with signs that say, HOME OF THE WORLD-FAMOUS MONSTER. Gift and souvenir shops are called "Nessie's." The Original Loch Ness Monster Visitor Centre in the village of Drumnadrochit advertises, "Find Nessie the Loch Ness Monster Here!" A travel Web site pronounces Drumnadrochit the "center of the Loch Ness Monster industry in Scotland." Nessie is obviously a very popular creature.

Worldwide Nessie

The famous beast of Loch Ness is so popular that a fan club was created in its honor. David Campbell founded the Official Loch Ness Monster Fan Club in 1996. He explains that when he had his own encounter with the monster, he had no idea where to report it. Also, no one was keeping any sort of record of Nessie sightings. Campbell decided to start the fan club, as well as a Web site. That way, he could compile people's stories about encounters with the monster and display them online. Nessie fans who join the club receive a badge, a membership certificate, and information about the loch and its mysteries.

A sculpture of Nessie greets visitors to Loch Ness. The monster draws thousands of tourists to the loch every year.

Je sais tou

L'AVENTURE HUMAINE DE TOUS LES TEM

TOUS LES MARDIS   N° 29   FRANCE 1,50 F BELGIQUE SUISSE

LE MONSTRE DU LOCH NESS EXISTE-T-IL ?

(page 16)

This French storybook shows the beast attacking fishermen on the loch.

The Loch Ness Monster

They also receive a Nessie stuffed toy and a supply of postcards. If they happen to see the monster, they can mail a postcard to Campbell. Visitors to the site can click on a webcam that shows Loch Ness. If the monster should decide to make an appearance, anyone with Internet access could see!

The fan club Web site is just one of hundreds of Web sites devoted to the Loch Ness Monster. Another popular one is Nessie's Grotto. It was created by Lois June Wickstrom and Jean Lorrah, both true Nessie fans. They visited Loch Ness in 1995 and

Although the monster's existence is questionable, Nessie remains very popular.

2001, and have been very interested in its mysterious beast ever since. Their site lists monster sightings, as well as photos taken by people who swear they have captured Nessie on film. The women have also written three books: *Nessie and the Living Stone, Nessie and the Viking Gold,* and *Nessie and the Celtic Maze.* People can order the books and other merchandise online. They can buy Nessie T-shirts, sweatshirts, coffee cups, baby bibs, and even an edible Nessie made of gingerbread. There is also a "Nessie's Maze" board game and a crossword puzzle. People can subscribe to the *Nessie's Grotto* newsletter, which gives readers the latest news about the Loch Ness Monster. A main feature of the newsletter is interviews with monster hunters.

MORE NESSIE MANIA

People can also find Loch Ness Monster toys, games, and trinkets on other Web sites. For instance, on the online auction site e-Bay, sellers offer a variety of items. Some are rather unusual. One item for sale was "The Monsters of Loch Ness" sewing pattern. Someone could use it to sew an entire family of stuffed Nessies. There were also books and old records, a Loch Ness Monster refrigerator magnet, figurines, and decanters, and a Nessie sea serpent designed for a flower garden. One seller offered "Nessie and Son," a green stuffed monster wearing a plaid tasseled hat and holding a baby monster. Another offered a green

A gift shop in Drumnadrochit sells stuffed Nessies of every size.

rubber Nessie squeaky toy. There were also many different buttons for sale. They said such things as "I Believe," "Nessie Lives," "Nessie Fan Club," and "I ♥ Nessie."

Nessie fans who travel to Loch Ness can find more monster merchandise than they could ever dream of. At Nessie's Gift Shop in Drumnadrochit, there are stuffed Nessies of every size. The shop sells Nessie chocolate candy and fudge, as well as infants' T-shirts that say, "I'm a wee monster."

A unique Nessie toy has been developed by a company called Takara. It is called "Radio Control

Incident at Loch Ness *is one of many movies about Nessie that Hollywood has produced in recent years.*

The Loch Ness Monster

Loch Ness." A toy monster floats in a pool or lake, and a handheld device controls its actions from as far as 60 feet (20m) away. The miniature beast's neck dips up and down in the water as it glides along the surface—just like some people have described Nessie.

Star Monster

Nessie is also the star character in dozens of books, as well as movies. The video *Scooby-Doo and the Loch Ness Monster* was released in 2004. It is the story of the Scooby-Doo gang's trip to Scotland, where they attempt to solve the mystery of the famous monster. Other films include *Loch Ness, Loch Ness Discovered, In Search of History: Loch Ness Monster,* and *Beneath Loch Ness.*

Nessie is also a television star. *The Family Ness* was a popular British children's cartoon show that aired during the 1980s. It featured a whole family of Nessies who lived in the depths of Loch Ness. Nobody believed in them except a brother and sister named Angus and Elspeth. The monster family included Baby-ness, the youngest; Careful-ness, the most cautious of the bunch; the oh-so-smart Clever-ness; and Eager-ness, the monster who was always willing to help. Grumpy-ness was a total grouch, and Ferocious-ness was a mean monster. Lovely-ness was beautiful, and Silly-ness always got into trouble. Speedy-ness zoomed about constantly, and Sporty-ness was good at water sports and liked to show off. In 2003, *The Family Ness* was released on videotape. Now, children all over the world can enjoy the antics of the monster family.

The Monster Lives On

Is Nessie real? Is there a strange, unknown creature that lives and thrives in the famous Scottish loch? Or is it simply a product of overactive imaginations, eyes playing tricks on people, or even deliberate deceptions? Someday the mystery may be solved. Then again, the truth may remain forever unknown. Dinsdale, the most devoted Nessie hunter of all time, died believing there was a creature in Loch Ness. He wrote of the lingering mystery: "I am not yet certain of the ending, but in the course of a decade I have watched the plot develop, and an almost empty stage slowly fill with characters—each with a part to play, a contribution to make, however small—to the whole tremendous story."[16] Nessie of Loch Ness may indeed be a myth, a legend, a fable. Yet to those who claim to have seen the elusive beast, it is every bit as alive and real as Scotland itself.

NOTES

Chapter 1: The Legend of Nessie

1. Quoted in Tim Dinsdale, *Loch Ness Monster.* London/Boston: Routledge & Kegan Paul, 1976, p. 18.
2. Quoted in Dick Raynor, "Loch Ness Investigation," www.lochnessinvestigation.org/history.html.
3. Quoted in F.W. Holiday, *The Great Orm of Loch Ness.* New York: W.W. Norton, 1969, p. 31.

Chapter 2: "Heavens Above! I've Actually Seen It!"

4. Quoted in "In Search of History: The Loch Ness Monster." New York: A&E Home Video, 1995.
5. Quoted in NOVA Online, "The Beast of Loch Ness," January 12, 1999. www.pbs.org/wgbh/nova/lochness/legend.html.
6. Dinsdale, *Loch Ness Monster,* p. 74.
7. Dinsdale, *Loch Ness Monster,* p. 79.
8. Quoted in Dinsdale, *Loch Ness Monster,* p. 93.
9. Quoted in NOVA Online, "The Beast of Loch Ness."
10. Quoted in NOVA Online, "The Beast of Loch Ness."
11. Quoted in NOVA Online, "The Beast of Loch Ness."

12. Quoted in NOVA Online, "The Beast of Loch Ness.

CHAPTER 3: REALITY OR MYTH?

13. Quoted in Jan Sundberg, "The Scientist Who [Believes] in Nessie." Global Underwater Search Team, 2003. www.bahnhof.se/~wizard/GUSTeng03/artiklar_henrybauer.html.
14. Quoted in Sandra Dick, "A Mystery That Can't Be Tamed," *Edinburgh Evening News,* July 18, 2003. http://news.scotsman.com/topics.cfm?tid=8&id=779862003.
15. Quoted in James Owen, "Loch Ness Sea Monster Fossil a Hoax, Say Scientists," *National Geographic News,* July 29, 2003. http://news.nationalgeographic.com/news/2003/07/0729_030729_lochness.html.
16. Dinsdale, *Loch Ness Monster,* p. 158.

GLOSSARY

cryptozoologist: Someone who studies creatures that may exist but are not accepted by formal science.

loch: The Scottish word for "lake."

natural phenomena: Events that occur in nature such as earthquakes and tornadoes.

plesiosaur: A large aquatic creature that lived hundreds of millions of years ago. Plesiosaurs lived in the seas when dinosaurs lived on land.

seiche: A large, standing wave in a closed body of water such as a lake or bay.

seismic: Shock waves produced within the Earth that can lead to earthquakes.

sonar: Technology that measures the size of an object using sound waves.

transponder: The sending and receiving device of sonar equipment.

wake: The track left by a moving body as it passes through water.

FOR FURTHER EXPLORATION

BOOKS

David C. Cooke and Yvonne Cooke, *The Great Monster Hunt*. New York: W.W. Norton, 1969. A book written by a married couple who traveled to Loch Ness, in search of the truth behind the famous monster.

Robert D. San Souci, *The Loch Ness Monster: Opposing Viewpoints*. San Diego: Greenhaven, 1989. An objective account of the facts and myths behind the beast of Loch Ness.

Holly Wallace, *The Mystery of the Loch Ness Monster*. Des Plaines, IL: Heinemann Library, 1999. Examines the history behind the Loch Ness Monster story, including eyewitness statements, possible explanations of what the beast is, and various attempts to discover and identify it.

VIDEO

"In Search of History: The Loch Ness Monster." New York: A&E Home Video, 1995. An excellent film about the Loch Ness Monster. It features interviews with people who claim to have seen the beast, as well as those who have hunted for it.

Web Sites

The Legend of Nessie (www.nessie.co.uk). A good site for Loch Ness Monster fans. It contains what the site creators describe as "documented evidence, film, first-hand accounts, stories, scientific studies and expeditions."

Loch Ness Information Site (www.loch-ness.co). This interesting site was created by Tony Harmsworth, who is considered an authority on the mystery of Loch Ness.

The Official Loch Ness Monster Fan Club (www.lochness.co.uk/fan_club). The online home of the official Nessie fan club. The site was started by Gary Campbell, one of the people who claims to have seen the Loch Ness Monster.

INDEX

About the Author

Peggy J. Parks holds a bachelor of science degree from Aquinas College in Grand Rapids, Michigan, where she graduated magna cum laude. She is a freelance author who has written more than thirty titles for Thomson Gale's KidHaven Press, Blackbirch Press, and Lucent Books imprints. Parks lives in Muskegon, Michigan, a town she says inspires her writing because of its location on the shores of Lake Michigan.